pumpkins pumpkins

PUMPKINS!

Celebrate autumn and Halloween with pumpkins! Decorating pumpkins, whether real or artificial, is a time-honored tradition for both autumn and Halloween. Cute, whimsical, scary, or sophisticated—any and all styles are welcome. Today's artificial pumpkins are so realistic-looking and come in all sizes, shapes, and colors. Many are even hollow, allowing them to be carved just like a real pumpkin. Here are a few tips for carving artificial pumpkins.

- While very similar to carving a real pumpkin, the faux pumpkins are a bit harder to cut/carve and the carving process produces quite a bit of dust. Cover your work surface. You may want to wear a dust mask.

- You can use pumpkin-carving knives and saws on an artificial pumpkin. A mini rotary cutting/drilling tool is handy, as well as some wood-carving tools. Be sure to wear safety glasses or goggles when using a power tool.

- After the cutting is done, sand the edges smooth with fine-grit sandpaper or an emery board. A sanding stick will get into those tight corners and angles. Wipe the pumpkin with a damp paper towel to remove sanding dust.

LEISURE ARTS, INC. • Maumelle, Arkansas

purple with spider

SHOPPING LIST

- large artificial pumpkin (about 11" diameter x 10" high)
- self-adhesive 5mm clear gemstone strips
- plastic spider (about 3" diameter)
- purple metallic shimmer spray paint
- silver metallic spray paint
- clear acrylic spray sealer
- hot glue gun & glue sticks

To decorate the Pumpkin:

1. Spray paint the pumpkin purple and the spider silver, allowing to dry between coats. Spray the pumpkin and spider with sealer.

2. Adhere gemstones to the spider. Adhere the gemstone strips to the pumpkin, placing the vertical strips first and curving the horizontal strips to create the spider's web. Use hot glue as necessary to hold gemstones in place. Glue the spider to the pumpkin.

black gemstone

SHOPPING LIST

- large artificial black pumpkin (about 9" diameter x 8" high)
- self-adhesive gemstone strips in varying sizes – clear, black, orange & purple
- hot glue gun & glue sticks

To decorate the Pumpkin:

Adhere gemstone strips to the pumpkin, varying the lengths and color placement. Use hot glue as necessary to hold gemstones in place.

TIP

Section off pumpkin lobes with gemstone strips of one color. Then, fill in the sections with the other colors.

flowers & pearls

SHOPPING LIST

- large artificial light-colored pumpkin (about 10" diameter x 10" high)
- self-adhesive gemstone stickers & pearl swirly stickers
- pearl brads & gemstones in varying sizes
- burlap flower petals in varying sizes & colors
- hot glue gun & glue sticks

To decorate the Pumpkin:

Plan the arrangement of the stickers, gemstones, brads, and flowers to best fit your pumpkin. To make each flower, layer a few burlap petals and secure with a pearl brad at the center. Adhere the pieces to the pumpkin, using hot glue as necessary to hold everything in place.

monogram

SHOPPING LIST

- large artificial pumpkin with sparkle finish (about 8 1/2" diameter x 8" high)
- 6" wide glitter tulle – four 12" lengths (2 black, 2 orange)
- black gemstones in varying sizes
- black acrylic paint & a paintbrush
- hot glue gun & glue sticks

To make the Monogram:

1. For your monogram, draw or print out a letter about 4 1/2" tall; cut out the letter. Use a pencil to draw around the letter on the pumpkin.

2. Paint the letter black.

3. Stack three tulle lengths; tightly tie the fourth length around the center of the tulle stack. Roughly trim the tulle short ends so they look ragged. Glue the tulle accent to the stem.

4. Glue the gemstones to the pumpkin, accenting the monogram.

Autumn carries more gold in its pockets than all the other seasons.

—Jim Bishop

glittered

SHOPPING LIST

- squatty artificial pumpkin (about 10" diameter x 6" high)
- glitter – orange, gold, beige & bronze
- jute twine
- clear acrylic spray sealer
- newspaper
- craft glue & a foam paintbrush
- hot glue gun & glue sticks

To decorate the Pumpkin:

1. Apply a heavy coat of craft glue to the sections of the pumpkin that you want to cover with orange glitter. Working over the newspaper, sprinkle orange glitter over the glue. Shake off any excess. Return the excess glitter to the original container. Allow to dry.

2. Repeat Step 1 with the gold, beige, and bronze glitters, allowing to dry between colors. Spray pumpkin with sealer.

3. Hot glue twine lengths between glitter colors.

> I would rather sit on a pumpkin and have it all to myself, than be crowded on a velvet cushion.
> —Henry David Thoreau

lace

SHOPPING LIST

- 2 small artificial pumpkins (about 6" diameter x 6" high each)
- pair of black lace tights
- black acrylic paint & a paintbrush
- two 18" lengths of 5/8" wide black ribbon
- yarn needle

To decorate each Pumpkin:

1. Paint the pumpkin stem black; allow to dry.
2. Cut off a tights leg about 7" above the toe. Place the pumpkin in the leg, centering the toe on the pumpkin bottom.
3. Thread a ribbon length through the yarn needle. Weave the ribbon in and out of the lace about 1/2" from the cut edge. Pull the ribbon ends to gather the tights leg around the pumpkin. Tie the ribbon in a bow and trim the ends. Tuck in the lace raw edges.

chalkboard

SHOPPING LIST

- large artificial pumpkin (about 10" diameter x 10" high)
- silver sparkle cardstock
- black chalkboard spray paint
- white chalk stick
- tracing paper
- hot glue gun & glue sticks

To make the Pumpkin:

1. Spray paint the pumpkin black, allowing to dry between coats.

2. Trace the bat patterns, page 15, onto tracing paper; cut out. Use the patterns to cut 1 of each size bat from silver cardstock. Crease the bat wings away from the body; curve the wings to look as though each bat were flying. Glue the bat bodies to the pumpkin.

3. Use the chalk stick to draw a design or write a message on the pumpkin.

When black cats prowl and pumpkins gleam, may luck be yours on Halloween.

fairy garden

SHOPPING LIST

- large artificial carvable pumpkin (about 11" diameter x 12" high)
- pumpkin-carving tools
- fine-grit sandpaper, sanding stick, or emery board
- fairy figurines & accessories (we used mini mushrooms, log slices, & a wooden bridge)
- green sheet moss & dyed Spanish moss
- artificial flowers & leaves
- gravel
- 15" square of thick polyester batting
- LED tea light
- hot glue gun & glue sticks

To make the Garden:

1. For front opening, draw a rounded-off square, about 8 1/2" x 7", on paper. Draw a rounded-top window shape about 3" x 3 1/2" on paper. Cut out the patterns. Use a pencil to draw around the patterns on the pumpkin front and sides.

2. Use the carving tools to cut out the front opening and windows. Smooth the cut edges.

3. Remove the stems from the flowers and leaves. Arrange and glue the flowers and leaves on the pumpkin as desired. Add a few mini mushroooms near the pumpkin stem.

4. Lay a bed of batting inside the pumpkin, spot gluing as necessary to create little hills and valleys. Cover the batting with sheet moss, spot gluing as necessary. Arrange and glue the fairies, accessories, gravel, and Spanish moss on the sheet moss. Place the tea light behind one of the accessories.

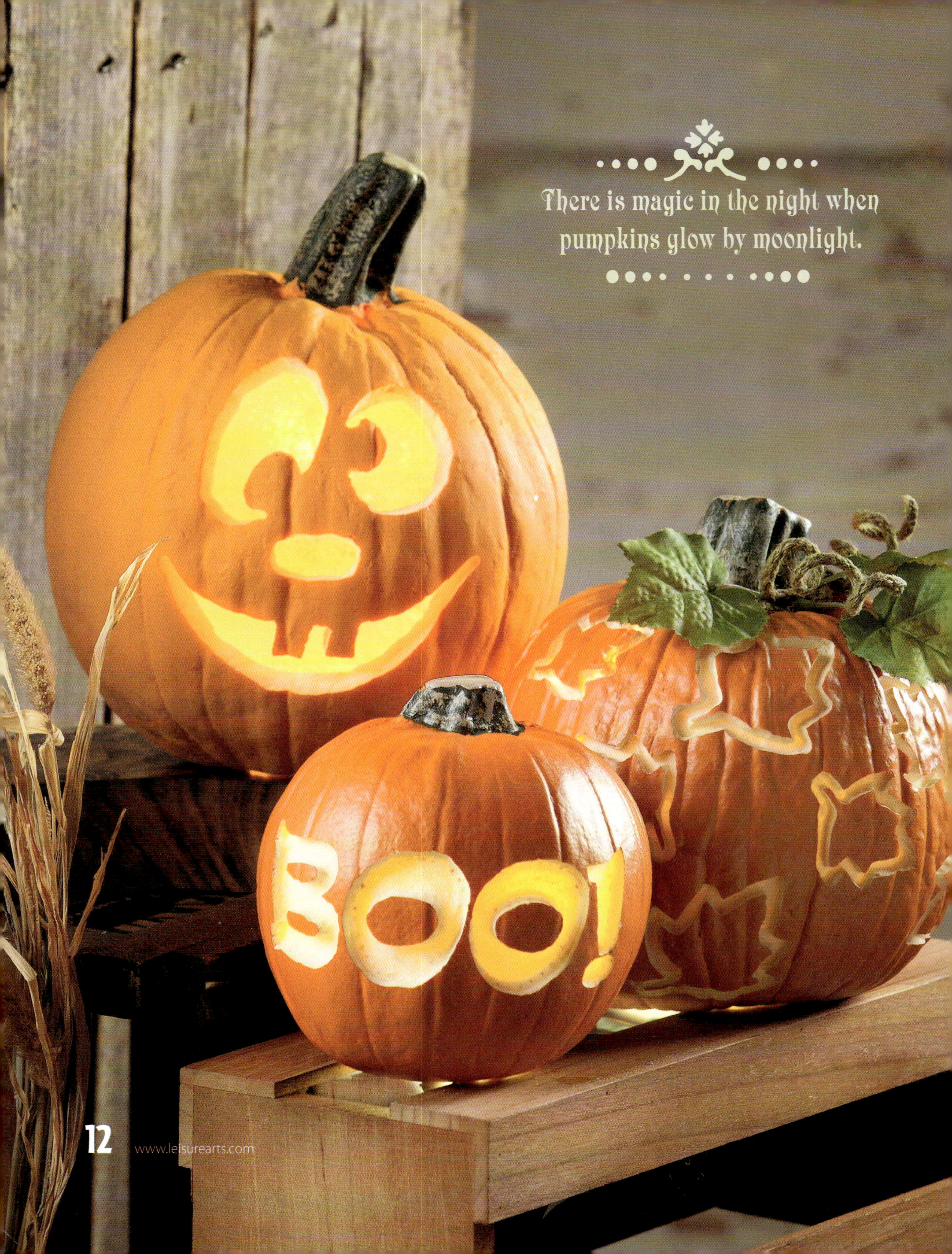

There is magic in the night when
pumpkins glow by moonlight.

funny face

SHOPPING LIST

- artificial carvable pumpkin (about 9" diameter x 9" high)
- pumpkin-carving tools
- fine-grit sandpaper, sanding stick, or emery board
- tracing paper
- LED tea light

To carve the Pumpkin:

1. If the pumpkin does not have a hole in the bottom for the tea light, draw around the tea light on the center bottom of the pumpkin. Use the carving tools to cut out the circle just beyond the drawn line; smooth the cut edges.
2. Trace the Funny Face patterns (page 16) onto tracing paper; cut out. Use a pencil to draw around the patterns on the pumpkin.
3. Cut out the facial features. Smooth the cut edges. Place the pumpkin over the tea light.

boo!

SHOPPING LIST

- small artificial carvable pumpkin (about 6" diameter x 6" high)
- pumpkin-carving tools
- fine-grit sandpaper, sanding stick, or emery board
- LED tea light

To carve the Pumpkin:

1. If the pumpkin does not have a hole in the bottom for the tea light, draw around the tea light on the center bottom of the pumpkin. Use the carving tools to cut out the circle just beyond the drawn line; smooth the cut edges.
2. Draw or print out "BOO!" on paper; cut out. Use a pencil to draw around the pattern on the pumpkin.
3. Cut the letters, being careful to not cut all the way through the pumpkin wall. Smooth the cut edges. Place the pumpkin over the tea light.

leaves

SHOPPING LIST

- artificial carvable pumpkin (about 7$^1/_2$" diameter x 6$^1/_2$" high)
- pumpkin-carving tools
- fine-grit sandpaper, sanding stick, or emery board
- 3 artificial leaves
- two 9" lengths of green 4mm wired jute rope
- tracing paper
- LED tea light
- hot glue gun & glue sticks

To carve the Pumpkin:

1. If the pumpkin does not have a hole in the bottom for the tea light, draw around the tea light on the center bottom of the pumpkin. Use the carving tools to cut out the circle just beyond the drawn line; smooth the cut edges.

2. Trace the leaf patterns (page 15) onto tracing paper; cut out. Use a pencil to draw around the patterns on the pumpkin, rotating the patterns and covering the entire pumpkin.

3. Cut the leaves, being careful to not cut all the way through the pumpkin wall. Smooth the cut edges.

4. For the tendrils, twist each green jute rope length around your finger. Glue the tendrils and leaves to the pumpkin. Place the pumpkin over the tea light.

patterns

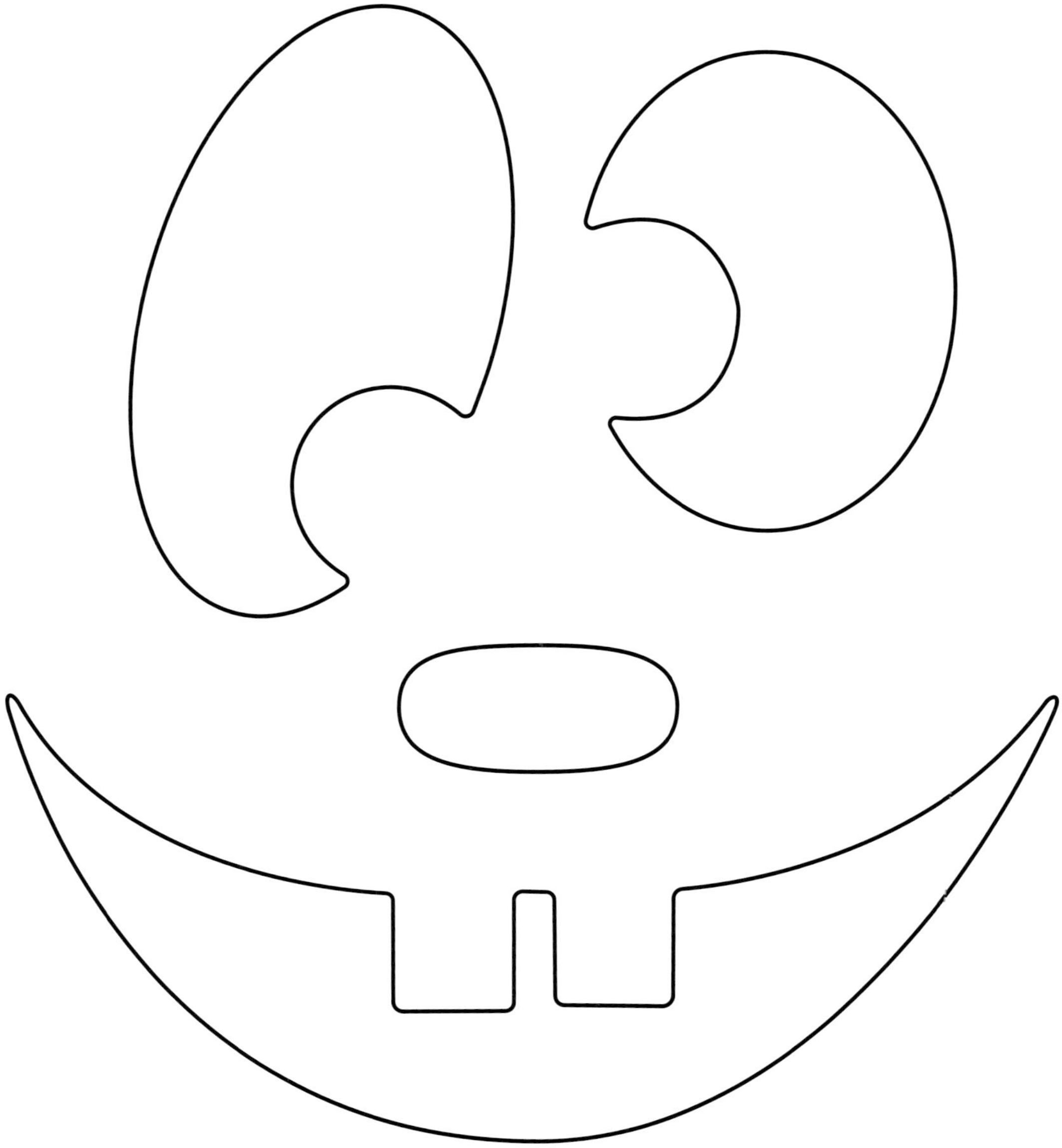

Production Team: Designer – Kelly Reider; Technical Writer – Mary Sullivan Hutcheson; Technical Associates – Lisa Lancaster and Jean Lewis; Editorial Writer – Susan Frantz Wiles; Senior Graphic Artist – Lora Puls; Graphic Artist – Cailen Cochran; Photostylist – Lori Wenger; Photographer – Jason Masters.